SUPERNATURAL
BUSINESS

Mike Floyd

CREATION
HOUSE
A STRANG COMPANY

SUPERNATURAL BUSINESS by Mike Floyd
Published by Creation House
A Strang Company
600 Rinehart Road
Lake Mary, FL 32746
www.creationhouse.com

Unless otherwise noted, all Scripture quotations are from the King James Version of the Bible.

Library of Congress Control Number: 2002116623

International Standard Book Number: 0-88419-972-X

Printed in the United States of America
08 09 10 11 12   8 7 6 5 4

If you're ready to make your business super-successful, using spiritual principles, you must read, re-read and then refer your friends to this brilliantly insightful, power-packed book. Mike Floyd is a close friend. Mike did what he says and shows you how you can too. You'll love it.

—Mark Victor Hansen
Co-creator, #1 *New York Times* best-selling series
Chicken Soup for the Soul®

Some books you read a little, lay down, then pick up later! Some books you don't even bother to pick up later! Then there are those very special books which come into your life and are so anointed you can't stop from the time you start until you are completely finished! Such is the book, *Supernatural Business*. Mike Floyd shares incredible principles of prosperity and tells entrepreneurs how to conduct business successfully on a godly basis. If you know people who want to succeed in business, help them by giving them a copy of this book. Everything in the book is exactly as he writes! It works!

—Charles and Frances Hunter
The Happy Hunters, Hunter Ministries

This book is a tremendous blessing to me, and I am sure it will be a great help to anyone building a business. Mike and Donna Floyd have been our friends for years, and they are some of the most generous, giving people I've ever met. They have realized that as they give, God gives back to them. He has opened the windows of heaven and blessed them abundantly! And I'm impressed by the wisdom God has given them. New ideas come easily to them because they seek God's face and His perfect will. As you apply the principles in this book, you will see the goodness of God and you will prosper. Thus, you will be enabled to further the gospel of the Lord Jesus Christ.

—Dodie Osteen
Co-founder, Lakewood Church, Houston, Texas

Acknowledgments

In developing the idea for this book, I credit first the Holy Spirit, and I also sincerely appreciate the help of my dear wife, Donna Kay, and other friends. In 1976, the revelation of the believer's authority and the fact that we have a covenant with God was unveiled to us. It was a shocking truth to face; during twenty-five years as a dedicated Christian, I had not realized that we have a personal covenant with Almighty God through His Son, Jesus Christ.

Contents

Chapter One

Beginnings

IT IS AN AWESOME FEELING TO REALIZE THAT YOU ARE A child of the Most High God, and that you are in personal covenant with Him. As a result, you are a partner with Almighty God, Creator of the universe.

There are no words in my vocabulary that are broad enough or sufficiently comprehensive to express my sincere amazement at this awe-inspiring truth. It was God's idea to be in covenant with His children.

This realization goes beyond the limits of my understanding. In 1976, when I began to comprehend this truth, it changed my entire life. Neither I nor my wife, Donna, have been the same since.

I truly believe I was born with an entrepreneurial spirit. As a boy, earning money one way or another was the norm. During the hot, sultry summer days spent in the small southern town of Marianna, Florida, where I grew up, I was always working on some business venture.

It seemed to me that earning money by selling a product or offering a service was the only way to approach employment. Because of this, there were many "great" business ventures around our home in my childhood. I sold parched or boiled peanuts, fruit from our pear tree and even cans of medicated salve. Of course, my dear mom was relegated to her kitchen boiling and parching peanuts for my business venture. In truth, our effort generated far more trouble than money.

Making money, at that time, was not my goal. The challenge was what motivated me.

One day a great advertisement appeared in *Popular Mechanics* magazine soliciting salesmen for medicated salve. The slick promotion convinced me that I could sell enough cans of Cloverine Medicated Salve to win all the terrific prizes shown in the ad. There was no doubt in my mind I could do it.

With Mom's help, I ordered a case of Cloverine Medicated Salve. Relatives were my first target market. Of course, grandparents, aunts and uncles purchased a token tin of the wonder ointment. Once they purchased their merchandise, a new target market was extremely elusive.

Again, Mom paid for my venture and bought my entire unsold inventory. Our family had enough medicated salve to last for years, with some left over.

The job that stands out most in my youth was working with my Uncle Ike on a small farm, grinding corn at twenty-five cents per tub. Revelation came quickly that the job could be subcontracted.

Subcontracting this work to my two cousins at fifteen cents per tub yielded a tidy net profit of ten cents per tub. That principle has stuck with me, even to this day.

You do not have to do all the work to get paid part of the money.

Subcontracting for a clear profit of ten cents per tub seemed to suit me better than actually doing the work for twenty-five cents per tub.

In continuing my career, the impressive enterprise of grass-cutting seemed the most likely venture to yield the highest profit. Many kids who were mowing lawns used the older-type push mower, but at my request, my uncle invested forty dollars in a power mower. Naturally, I had a plan to pay him back; although I don't remember him ever letting me repay the loan.

Working by the hour seemed to limit my production; therefore, the only pricing I would give to customers was to contract their yard jobs for a set amount instead of working for an hourly rate. A select group of regular customers developed who wanted their grass cut every two weeks. I did not know at the time that this was God's favor working in my life.

My mother taught me at an early age the privilege of tithing. She taught me to give ten cents of each dollar because it was God's, and He would make the balance go further. Even today I consider it a genuine blessing and a privilege to tithe. I noticed that other kids around my age were picking cotton and making about seventeen dollars per week. Some were loading watermelons and making about the same amount of money. On many of my workdays, I would earn ten to twelve dollars and still have time to go to the city swimming pool in the afternoon.

By the time I was thirteen, I had learned several basic principles: tithing works; pick your customers right; and if you want to swim in the afternoon, you have got to start cutting grass early in the morning.

The grass-cutting business was phased out after its due season, and I began to work with my father in his radio and appliance business. Television was just making its debut in our area, and it was an exciting time as a complete new industry was dawning. It was thrilling just to *see* a television. Even more rousing, though, was seeing a picture occasionally appear on those old boxes that were mostly filled with snowy shadows. No one realized the impact television was to have on our entire society—for good and bad.

When the military recruiters tested me in high school, my scores were very high in electronics because of the training I had received while working with my father. Shortly after graduation, though I cannot remember all the reasons at the time, I made a choice to enlist in the U.S. Air Force rather than attend the junior college located only a mile or so from our home. I received extensive training in aerospace electronics, and working on sophisticated equipment became my normal routine. After leaving the military, I sought a career in aerospace electronics and was employed by several firms over the years. While working with a large aerospace firm on the mammoth Apollo/Saturn project at Kennedy Space Center, I really began to question my career direction, even though each of my employment experiences was a blessing. Most of us working for the "man on the moon" project loved it. My search for something more was not out of dissatisfaction, but out of a search for something I discerned was missing in my life.

The foremost consideration in my mind was to please God. When you really want to know God's will for your life, He will reveal it to you. Of course, He usually will reveal only what we need for that given time.

While working on the aerospace projects, Donna and I continued to tithe on all of our income, and we enjoyed continued financial blessings. These blessings seemed to be above and beyond what folk experienced who we knew did not tithe.

God spoke to my heart one day (I do not mean I heard Him with my ears, but I heard Him in my mind) as I wrote my tithe check. He asked, "Why are you so tight with me?" In response, I countered, "How am I tight with you, Lord?"

Though I did not hear a response, God impressed a revelation into my understanding. It was the principle of sowing and reaping.

When you consider the fact that you receive back in the same measure in which you give, only multiplied, it looks different. I had not considered a profound principle of the Word of God—the principle of sowing and reaping. I was paying exactly one-tenth of all I received, even to the cent. I realized God was saying to me, "You will limit me in your life if you stop at exactly ten percent."

If you do not want God to be tight with you, do not be tight with Him. God wants to bless us, but He cannot if we do not allow Him to do so. We immediately started rounding out our checks to the nearest dollar. How generous we thought we were!

Before long, we were seeing little "cost of living" increases in our paychecks. One day we thought, *Why not round off the thirteen-dollar check to fifteen dollars?* A little later the thought crossed our minds, *We have been giving fifteen dollars. Why not twenty dollars?* As a little more time passed, the question became, *We have been giving twenty dollars. Why not give twenty-five dollars?*

It was evident that the more we gave, the more we had to give and the more we had left over. Even when we went to purchase items, we got great deals every time. It was somewhat uncanny to sit back and observe what was happening. Later we would realize it truly was the blessing that rests upon those who tithe.

It is the truth that you cannot outgive God, but most have never tried to do so. The increase we started then—more than thirty years ago—continues today.

You might ask the question, "Does tithing really work?" The answer will come loudly, "It really, really does in many, many ways."

In the early days of my career, a question stayed in my mind, *Where will you be in ten years?* It was an appropriate question, and the answer seemed obvious. *Well, if you continue your education and get your degree in electrical engineering, you will probably be chief systems engineer in your department.* That was a pretty good position in the company where I worked. It was a position of exciting responsibilities, and good pay could easily be expected.

The next question I faced seemed more difficult to answer, *Is this really what you want to do with the rest of your life?* The answer, while more difficult, seemed clear. Although this was a good career, I did not believe it was the right career choice for me.

Even though something is good, it might not be good or right for you. There are many very talented men and women in similar positions who are called of God to be there, but you may not be one of them.

I know God sometimes places us in the "valley of decision." The question we often ask as we face the task of making a decision is something akin to, "Is it a good opportunity?" However, the question we really ought to ask is, "Is this the right choice for me?"

No was the honest answer to my dilemma. I wanted to do something that involved people, and lots of them. I also wanted to do something that would reward my efforts and affect my income and relationships with people.

One of the jobs at the space center was to babysit the missile. It was rather dull, as there were no duties other than to monitor tank pressures. One evening while on babysitting duty, I decided to form my own company. My idea was simply to find unique products and market them.

Of course this was a big, new, exciting venture that I wrote out on a large desk-calendar sheet. At least it was big in my mind. Donna and I prayed over it, worked on it as a team, and dedicated our ideas to God. The principles our venture was to be founded on were solid biblical precepts. *Despise not the day of small beginnings.* Most great projects and endeavors start small. If they are of God, most will not stay small for very long. Little did I know that God was preparing to raise up a *supernatural business* through us.

Many would ask, "What is a *supernatural business?*" and "How does a *supernatural business* differ from any other business?"

Many thought-provoking questions have been asked about a supernatural business, and most of them will be answered in this book. To understand the basic idea, let us look at the word *supernatural.* Webster's dictionary offers an unexaggerated description, "Existing or occurring outside the normal experience or knowledge of man; not explainable by the known forces or laws of nature; specifically, of, involving or attributed to God."

My definition of supernatural reveals the fact that God is involved in each area of our business, and we run it on His principles.

Chapter Two

Foundations

HOW DOES GOD RAISE UP A SUPERNATURAL BUSINESS?
It is really simple. He first builds a strong foundation. This does not happen overnight, or even over the period of a year. It is an extensive project that develops a leader into a pacesetter whose confidence lies in no man but entirely on God and the principles of His Word.

It is just as important to find out what *not* to do as it is to find out what *to* do. I know personally that finding out what *to* do is simple. What *not* to do usually comes through experience and sometimes can be very painful.

Remember Joseph? He was a dreamer. Genesis tells the story of Joseph's dream.

> And Joseph dreamed a dream, and he told it his brethren, and they hated him yet the more. And he said unto them, "Hear, I pray you, this dream which I have dreamed: For, behold, we were binding sheaves in the field, and lo, my sheaf arose and also stood upright,

and behold, your sheaves stood round about, and made obeisance to my sheaf."

And his brethren said to him, "Shalt thou indeed reign over us? Or shalt thou indeed have dominion over us?" And they hated him yet the more for his dreams and for his words.

And he dreamed yet another dream and told it his brethren and said, "Behold, I have dreamed a dream more, and, behold, the sun and the moon and the eleven stars made obeisance to me."

And he told it to his father and to his brethren, and his father rebuked him and said unto him, "What is this dream that thou hast dreamed? Shall I and thy mother and thy brethren indeed come to bow down us to thee to the earth?"

And his brethren envied him, but his father observed the saying.

—GENESIS 37:5–11

Joseph was a visionary in training. He had the favor of his father and thought everyone would be excited about his vision. They were not.

People, in general, probably won't be impassioned about your dreams and visions either. Many are jealous when confronted with someone who is moving out of mediocrity and small-thinking mentality.

Joseph had a vision, but he needed training.

Sometimes God's training program is extensive and long. In a day when our society wants everything instantly, we sometimes balk at God's plan, but He knows the foundation has to be laid. This foundation must be deep and strong to withstand the wind and waves of life, and Satan, the enemy of our souls. If you are going to be a servant of God and work to build something worthwhile in His kingdom, you should plan on adopting the foundational principles we will cover in this book.

If any of your building can be shaken apart, it will be. This is evidenced in Hebrews 12:27: "And this word, yet once more, signifieth the removing of those things that are shaken, as of things that are made, that those things which cannot be shaken may remain." God is going to be glorified by doing things for which man cannot take the credit. There are several "foundation stones" for building a supernatural business.

The first foundation stone is *integrity*. What is integrity? Again, we borrow from Webster. Integrity is "the quality or state of being of sound moral principle; uprightness, honesty, and sincerity." You cannot oversee a supernatural business without complete dedication to integrity. Even when no one would know, everything has to operate by and on this principle.

Later, we will be dealing with *trust*. If your client is going to trust you, your relationship has to be based on complete commitment to this foundational stone. If you do not have deep personal integrity based on God's Word, eventually your lack will cause inordinate trouble and distress. You will be tested on this principle. Decide that your actions are going to be in alignment with God's Word, no matter the immediate or future cost.

You may have to reconsider previous methods and habits in your business to arrive at the place where God wants you. Once you decide that you are going to operate in integrity, the Holy Spirit will help you. I can remember deciding not to provide any materials to promote alcohol, cigarettes, the lottery, other gambling ventures or anything that would displease the Holy Spirit. Right away, a large oil company wanted me to manufacture display items to advertise many of their commodities—one of which was cigarettes.

I rationalized that it was just business, so we created the items. It seemed like it did not matter, and from all appearances, it looked as if we were going to go great-guns with this company. They invited me to visit their national headquarters with my contact person in the state.

Just before I was to visit the national office and be introduced to the vice president and others at this titan corporation, they retired my contact person, and the connection went out the door. Even small decisions that appear to be commercially acceptable can be deal-killers with God.

My next experience in the area of integrity was the response we received from an advertisement we ran in *The Wall Street Journal*. The only credible response we got was from a hotel owner in Las Vegas. He wanted to advertise his hotel all over the area with small billboard-type signs. While talking with him I learned that he wanted to promote the gambling aspect of his business. I simply explained to him why we could not produce the signs and declined the order.

In a supernatural business it becomes necessary to take a stand for the things you know are right.

Many years have come and gone since we decided to honor our commitment to not design promotional materials for certain products or businesses. Today we service several major national accounts, and not one of them needs any product that promotes alcohol, cigarettes, gambling or anything else offensive to God. The Holy Spirit can lead you to the customers who either do not want to promote offensive materials or customers who are in a field that does not deal with distasteful matters—things that stain the soul.

Chapter Three

Principles

IN ORDER FOR A PERSON TO HAVE A SUPERNATURAL business, it is imperative that the enterprise be founded on solid "Word of God" principles.

God runs the universe through His Word that controls the laws of nature. His Word upholds all things. The apostle Paul shows this in Hebrews 1:3: "Who being the brightness of His glory and the express image of His person and upholding all things by the word of His power, when He had by Himself purged our sins, sat down on the right hand of the Majesty on high."

Therefore, we know that when we operate on His principles and His laws, we will get His results. Many of these principles will be covered in detail in later chapters.

With regard to business, the desire to own not just any business but a supernatural business has to be based on proper motives. If you want to build a great name for yourself or accumulate a large estate for your glory, this is not the book that will show you how to do that. My instructions and testimonies in this book are for the Christian businessman or woman whose heart's desire is to fulfill a call and purpose in life and to further the kingdom of God on this earth.

Principle 1—The Golden Rule

One overriding principle you will notice throughout this book is a simple but powerful one: *Treat others exactly like you want to be treated.*

Jesus explains this in Matthew 7:12: "Therefore all things whatsoever ye would that men should do to you, do ye even so to them; for this is the law and the prophets."

You cannot believe what the Golden Rule will do in the area of customer service. I make it a practice to observe the kind of service other companies give. Often I am amazed, not at the good service but at the lack of any service at all.

Unfortunately, this seems to be a trend. I know that companies with little or no customer service do not realize that what they're doing is actually costing them future sales. The average person will not register a complaint with the management, but will tell at least ten others how badly he was treated. Scripture tells us that a brother offended is harder to win back than a walled castle. The same principle applies in the business arena. A customer offended is harder to win back than a walled castle, and you may never win him back, no matter the advertising dollars you spend or the value of your product.

Our largest client today came to us as a direct result of our application of the Golden Rule principle. Several years ago I received a call from a gentleman named Chuck, who previously had been a representative of one of our clients in the Northeast. He had called and asked if I could come to Philadelphia to discuss setting up a program for a new franchise company, so I agreed and we met.

After our discussion, I felt the concept he proposed would not work, but I chose to treat it like I would a million-dollar account. I handled this project with the greatest respect I could because that's the way I would like to be treated if I were in his position.

We do not know when God is setting up something big for us. It may appear small and insignificant, or it may be a test to find out our true motives and attitudes. Before God can trust you with something big, He wants to know if you can handle it.

I did a little work for Chuck's project and did not get paid for six months. I just sent him a statement and prayed over it. I could have sent threatening letters suggesting legal action and turn him over to the collection agencies. In my opinion, collection agencies are referred to in the New Testament as "tormentors." Many times I have seen companies turn over good clients to such agencies when they get behind with their payments. The relationship between company and client may have produced tens of thousands of dollars in business in the past, but now that the client has fallen behind, the previous relationship is all but forgotten. I made a conscious choice not to subject this young company to such torment.

How sad it is to be so narrow-minded and shallow that no value is put on past or future relationships with clients. That is the normal business practice when dealing with carnally minded people—Christian or not.

Having been both the debtor and the lender at one time or another, I can empathize with both sides of this issue.

In this case the company eventually paid us but in the end went bankrupt.

It wasn't until a couple of years later that I found out what happened to my friend Chuck. Early one morning in my wife's prayer time, God spoke to her heart that I was to receive an important telephone call that day. I was not feeling very spiritual and brushed it off.

During the day, I was reminded of my commitment to help a widow get a car. I spent some time helping her but felt much of my time was being wasted

At about 3 P.M. Donna answered the telephone and said there was a lady asking for the representative that handled a specific account that happened to be one of the largest fast-food chains in the world. I indicated that Donna should tell the lady that the gentleman she had requested was in, and I would take the call in my office. I can't recall if we had any full-time employees then, but I know we didn't have more than one.

The lady on the other end of the conversation was a representative of one of the largest advertising agencies in the world. She spent about 45 minutes describing her need and was delighted to find that our company could handle the project. At the end of our conversation, I asked her how she had heard of us. I was shocked when she said that a man named Chuck, who now was working with her company, referred her to us.

I could hardly believe my ears. The same man to whom I had shown favor and treated with great respect had passed my name to a representative handling a project for one of the largest companies in the world.

As of this writing, this client is our largest multi-million-dollar client and is growing every day. I truly believe if I had gotten ugly about the few hundred dollars Chuck's company owed us and treated him badly, I would have never known the potential business we would have missed.

How tragic to not treat folks like we would like to be treated! We never know the opportunities missed and the blessings we will never get to enjoy.

Principle 2—God's Wisdom

Man's wisdom is foolishness to God, and God's wisdom is foolish to worldly minded men. In 1 Corinthians 3:18–19 we find this principle: "Let no man deceive himself. If any man among you seemeth to be wise in this world, let him become a fool, that he may be wise. For the wisdom of this world is foolishness with God. For it is written, He taketh the wise in their own craftiness."

Receiving God's wisdom requires the simple recognition that God knows all, is aware of all, and knows the solution to all.

Too often we limit the application of this wisdom to church situations and really do not think that God knows about technical or business subjects. But He knows who needs what product or service and even where they are. He can reveal to you who to see and when to see them.

I stand in absolute awe of God, Creator of the universe and all that exists. To know we have access to the vast array of His blessings really stretches my understanding. I am equally amazed at those who reject this great wisdom and knowledge—all to their detriment.

Principle 3—Important Things First

Often we are absorbed with the urgency of life, and consequently we forget what is really important. If we deal with important matters, many of the urgent issues will never require our attention.

Once I heard an illustration where a lecturer began to fill a huge jar with large stones. After filling it to the top, he asked, "Is it full?" The reply was *yes*. However, the lecturer began to put gravel in between the large stones.

By the time he asked again, the audience had realized it was possible to put smaller things around the larger. After the gravel, he put in sand, and after the sand he filled the jar with water.

He then asked, "What principle did this illustrate?"

Most answered, "It's not full 'til it's full."

The illustration showed there was a more important principle at work: *If you put in the large or important things first, you will always find a place for smaller or less important things.* If you put in sand or smaller things first, the large or more important things will not fit in later.

I have paid a high price throughout my life because of my failure to follow this simple principle. It takes discipline to do the important when the urgent is calling out loudly for attention. It is easy to procrastinate on the important things until they are lost in time and become just a vague memory. How sad it is to neglect the important because of distraction by the unimportant. This could be *the* major hindrance to many people fulfilling the call and destiny for their lives.

Principle 4—Act: When You Know What to Do, Do It

When you know what to do, do it.

Procrastination, or putting off till tomorrow what should be done today, is the greatest thief I know of for the Christian. The Bible teaches: "Today is the day of salvation." One of the greatest tricks of Satan is to tell people they have plenty of time. Do not worry today; you will have plenty of time tomorrow. The truth is that we are not guaranteed tomorrow. Tomorrow is in the hand of God. Most opportunities are given to us as windows that are opened for only a brief period of time—sometimes very brief. In some cases those moments are fleeting, allowing for just one choice.

More than twenty-five years later, I am still reminded of how I missed the will of God concerning the purchase of a radio station. Donna and I were thirsty for a real move of God in Tallahassee, Florida, our hometown. The spiritual atmosphere seemed dry and stagnant. Our hunger ran deep, and we were committed to doing anything we could to invite His powerful presence to our city.

While passing through a different city I heard beautiful praise music and prayed that God would bring that to Tallahassee in the form of a Christian radio station.

As I prayed, I heard the gentle voice of the Holy Spirit say to me, "I am looking for someone to bring a station on."

I quickly responded that He had found His man. I was very excited and began to look for a frequency and to inquire as to cost and other matters related to starting a radio station. Everywhere I turned I seemed to run into a dead end. I felt somewhat confused and wondered if I truly had heard from God.

Within a couple of years, though, we received a prophetic word that God had a 100,000-watt station ready and that He would present it to us. Through rather unusual circumstances, we found out about a station that was up for sale—a 50,000-watt FM with a 10,000-watt AM affiliate. Upon closer examination, we found that the station actually had permission to operate at 100,000 watts, and the transmitter had been purchased already.

When we inquired about the price, we found that two partners, one of which we knew casually, had joint ownership. The other was president of a large company that builds homes nationwide.

I communicated with the owners for several weeks,

and during that time I had a vision for the use of these stations. We wanted the FM to bless the city with beautiful praise and worship music during the day and to minister to the lonely and destitute at night. The AM was to be a dynamic, contemporary youth station.

The owners wanted one million dollars for both stations.

This seemed an impossible figure to me, and I began to try to figure out how we might come up with the money to pay for the stations. I knew it was God's will for us to own the stations, but I didn't know how to get around the price tag.

The real problem was not the money, though. It was my failure to say three little words during my conversations with the owners, "I'll take them." Until I said those words, I didn't need any money. Once those three words were spoken, we could have met to work out the details.

You might say, "Well, you didn't know if it was going to work out." No, I didn't know, but I do know there was no way it was going to work out until I said those three words. Because of my failure to say them, I have no idea how many souls would have been saved and how many people the Word of God broadcast from those stations would have blessed.

When you know what to do, do it. I knew God had brought these stations to us, and I knew He had a plan, but I did not do all I could do.

The value of these stations now is more than five million dollars. Even though I don't believe we would have ever sold them, their financial value alone has increased tremendously over the past twenty-five years. I have long since asked God to forgive me for failing to act when I knew I should have acted, but that will not change the fact that some people probably will not be in heaven who would have been had I acted.

I have had to choose to move past this failure. To camp out in memory of this failure would have hindered the future and God's work in and through me.

Principle 5—Don't Turn or Look Back

We can never rewind and change our lives. We must learn our lessons and press forward. The apostle Paul gave some good counsel from his own life in Philippians 3:13–14: "Brethren, I count not myself to have apprehended: but this one thing I do, forgetting those things which are behind, and reaching forth unto those things which are before, I press toward the mark for the prize of the high calling of God in Christ Jesus."

We can waste much time reliving the past. Mentally reliving failures or victories already written in the sands of time will hold you back from fulfilling God's purpose for your life. Gain wisdom and insight from both failure and victory, and move forward in your life, business or ministry.

We cannot change the past, but we can certainly influence the future.

One minister said that we have large windshields and small rear view mirrors to reflect God's attitude toward the past. We need to keep one eye open on the past, but not dwell there.

Recently I went to a grocery store and came across a woman we had known from a church we attended more than twenty years ago. When we were there, her husband, Dan, had found out he had brain tumors. He had a lengthy illness and was not expected to live. We moved and never did find out what happened to him. In the store, the woman seemed very stressed and troubled. When I recognized her, I asked her what was wrong. She replied, "It hurts so bad, and I miss him so much." Assuming her husband had died years ago and she was grieving for someone else, I begin to counsel with her. When I asked her for whom she was grieving, she looked shocked and replied, "Dan, of course."

I inquired if Dan had died recently. Once again she looked shocked and said he had died more than twenty years ago. Compassion welled up within me as I realized she was living with this extreme hurt many years after her husband's death. It seemed as if her grief was as fresh as if he had passed away just the day before. Because she was tormented with the past, Satan had robbed this lady's family and friends of a very special person—herself.

Whatever it takes to move beyond the past is worth all your efforts.

This also has a practical application in the business world. Businesses that can't move out of the past are doomed to failure. Using outdated methods and equipment in today's world will not produce the results you want. Always let the future be your pull.

Recently I was on a small stretch of the classic American highway—Route 66. On this stretch I saw the remains of old hotels, restaurants and attractions. All brought a touch of nostalgia. All the things I saw were great for the forties, fifties and sixties, but not for today.

Things change, people change. We cannot live in the past and expect a harvest in the future.

If a business can't move into the future and out of the past, it will become a relic. You and I both could name several businesses that were large and extremely popular, and we thought they would last forever. However, many don't even exist today because they would not or could not change.

If you're going to have a supernatural business, you are going to have to think future. Anticipating the future and preparing for it will cause you to prosper more than you can imagine.

Guess who knows the future—your partner, the Holy Spirit.

I can remember when our business put in its first fax machine. What a modern convenience! We were ahead of most when we insisted on purchasing a plain paper fax. It cost a lot in those days, but it was well worth it.

When making any kind of purchase, I always ask three things: What does it cost? What is its value, and what will it cost if we don't purchase it?

Now we are sending most correspondence by e-mail, which is beginning to make the fax machine obsolete.

Continuing change is a constant for the believer who has a supernatural business.

Principle 6—Always Say *No* to Lack

Lack is an enemy. Say *no* to lack as you would any other temptation. Say *no* in words, actions and attitudes.

God has given you all things that pertain to life and godliness. In 2 Peter 1:3, Peter, a disciple who lacked a firm commitment in a time of testing, tells us: "According as His divine power hath given unto us all things that pertain unto life and godliness through the knowledge of Him that hath called us to glory and virtue."

To be "lack-oriented" will cause a delay in moving forward. If God has approved your plan of action, He also has made provision for it.

Any time we see lack, God sees abundance. This is evident in Luke 9:12–17:

> And when the day began to wear away, then came the twelve, and said unto Him, Send the multitude

> away, that they may go into the towns and country round about, and lodge, and get victuals: for we are here in a desert place. But He said unto them, Give ye them to eat. And they said, We have no more but five loaves and two fishes; except we should go and buy meat for all this people. For they were about five thousand men. And He said to his disciples, Make them sit down by fifties in a company. And they did so, and made them all sit down. Then He took the five loaves and the two fishes, and looking up to heaven, He blessed them, and brake, and gave to the disciples to set before the multitude. And they did eat, and were all filled: and there was taken up of fragments that remained to them twelve baskets.

Jesus had been teaching the multitudes for several days when He instructed the disciples to feed them. The disciples saw lack and wanted to send the people home hungry. Jesus saw abundance and commanded that the people be fed.

Reflecting their "lack" mentality, the disciples said, "We don't have anything, and there is no place to buy anything. We only have five loaves and two fishes." Of course, in man's eyes, that's not enough to feed five thousand.

Notice the disciples are speaking lack while Jesus is preparing to feed the multitudes. Many times I have found God speaking abundance in my own life and for the life of me, I could not see anything but lack. In such cases, we have to ask God to open our eyes to the opportunities and to reveal the abundance around us. It will not appear until we begin to act on God's word for this specific occasion.

I have often preached a sermon called "What you need is in your house." I learned its value some time ago when I was scheduled to attend a client's meeting in San Francisco. I had already spent several thousand dollars for the meeting, and the airline ticket cost an excessive amount. Frankly, I really did not want to spend the money and in fact, did not have the money.

I called the client and informed him I was not going to attend the meeting. I sensed quite a bit of disappointment and felt bad for cancelling. As I sought to justify not attending the meeting, I suddenly remembered my sermon, "What you need is in your house." I looked in my briefcase and found some old frequent flier statements.

The airline had long since gone out of business, but its frequent flier program was taken over by another airline. I called and was informed that my mileage was more than enough for my round trip ticket to San Francisco. Had I not learned the principle of thinking abundance, I would have just tossed the frequent flier mileage statements in the trash and not thought anything more about it.

If we are convinced of God's ability to meet our needs, even when we feel lack because of our circumstances, only then can we fulfill the call of God on all our lives. Historically, men have always thought they did not have enough to do what God wanted them to do. If you find yourself feeling this way at times, don't feel too bad, because you're in great company. The Bible tells of many great men and women who didn't think they had "enough" to do God's will.

Principle 7—Goals

Make detailed plans to succeed.

Failure is not an option or a consideration. Failure is not to be factored into our plans. We should plan to win every battle and set our goals so high that it takes God to put us over the top.

God wants you to succeed! If God does not fail, you cannot fail! As long as we are in Him, that is, in Jesus Christ, we know of a certainty we are going to win. Sometimes it looks like we do fail. However, if you continue to hold on to the truth, in the end, you will succeed.

We feed most failure with our words. We give up with our voices because of our circumstances. When we give up with our voices and release our authority to someone other than Almighty God, we can suffer failure and defeat.

If you find yourself in this position, it's time to repent and ask God to forgive you. Ask Him to put you back on track and start over again.

A friend of mine was flying back from overseas. He had a connecting flight in London, and when he arrived, the flight had already departed. He was told to return the next evening.

He overslept and arrived just in time to see the large jumbo jet taxi from the gate. He asked the agent if anything could be done and was informed there was not.

He decided to take his case to a Higher Power and started to pray in the Spirit. A little while later, two airline officials ran up to him and told him to follow them, and they proceeded to escort him to a waiting car and onto the airplane on the tarmac.

The rear door was open, and he was escorted onto the plane and up to first class. He was treated like royalty and to this day, doesn't know who they thought he was. Evidently they thought he was some celebrity.

God can cause extreme favor when we need it to override circumstances that are contrary to His Word.

Principle 8—Just Say No

When *no* is the right answer, then say *no*. Often there is strong pressure to say *yes* to a seemingly good thing. It may be a good opportunity, but not the right one. Just say *no* when *no* is required.

Excuses are not necessary; decide, and stick with it. Of course, when *yes* is the right answer, we should simply say *yes*. The quicker you learn to say *no* when *no* is required, the quicker your business will become focused and start to enjoy success.

When we respond with a *no*, many expect to hear an explanation for why we said *no*. A lot of sales people will try to take a different approach after hearing *no*. I usually do not enter into a discussion once I have said *no*. Continuing dialogue after a quality decision will give an opportunity for a right decision to be changed to a wrong decision. The Bible is very clear on this as we see in James 5:12: "But above all things, my brethren, swear not, neither by heaven, neither by the earth, neither by any other oath: but let your yea be yea; and your nay, nay; lest ye fall into condemnation."

I once ordered a new luxury automobile. I knew the one I wanted and ordered it exactly like I wanted it. It was to be several weeks before it came in. I got a call from the dealership advising me that the car I had ordered was not in, but they had one very similar.

I went and looked at the car, rationalizing it would be close enough. But once I drove off the parking lot, I realized I had made a mistake. The car immediately had a problem with the air conditioning, so I took it to the shop for repair. Meanwhile, the dealership called and informed me that the owner had reconsidered and wanted to cancel the deal. I informed them that the keys were in the car, and it was already in their repair shop.

This was my opportunity to get out of a deal I knew was not right. But a few days later, the dealership called again and said they would take the deal after all. Because I was impatient and didn't want to wait, I went and picked up the car once again. In the next few years almost every part in the car failed or malfunctioned. I learned a hard lesson about my yea being yea and my nay being nay.

Principle 9—No Deception

God does not approve of deception in business or ministry.

We have to be sincere and operate without deception in every area of business. To attempt to look "big" when we are small will preempt the contacts and trust God puts into our lives.

Trying to present yourself as something you are not is a scam, and "faking it until you make it" will not work in the supernatural business. Perhaps the most valuable asset we have in our corporation is our client's trust. This has come through many years of being honest with our customers. Though most of our clients are giants in their field, they operate in honesty and integrity. They want straight answers, even though they might not be the answers they want to hear. Deception will cause a loss of trust, and when trust is gone there is no basis upon which to conduct business.

My very good friend and prayer partner had a satellite business and was being hurt by his competitors because they were selling illegal satellite receivers. All the other dealers in the area were giving free programming to their clients because, with illegal receivers, they did not have to pay for the programming.

My friend was very discouraged and went to God in prayer and asked God to judge between him and his competitors. Not long thereafter he received a call from the FBI office in town requesting to talk with him. He had no idea why they would want to talk with him and was very surprised about the subject of the conversation. The FBI indicated they had raided the distributor that was selling the illegal devices and inquired as to the identity of any dealers using the illegal devices. The distributor told the FBI that it would be easier to tell them who did not use the devices and that would be only one dealer, my friend.

Several months later the FBI asked my friend if he would allow his business to serve as a "turn-in point" for illegal receivers. The FBI set up an open account for him with the manufacturer for new receivers. A letter was sent to all owners of illegal receivers, giving them 30 days to turn in the illegal units, obtain a legal one from my friend, or face a fine and imprisonment.

For the next several months there was a line of customers at his place of business buying receivers and subscribing to programming. I would never have guessed God would use the FBI to right the wrongs my friend was encountering. Integrity and honesty does pay, and it will pay in your life, too.

Chapter Four

Favor of God and Man

G OD'S WORD PROMISES US THAT WHEN OUR WAYS please the Lord, we will have favor with God and man. This favor is vital when God is using you to build a supernatural business.

Throughout biblical history God used this methodology to bring blessings. God does not change in character or principle. If He used this approach with Abraham, Moses and other men and women of God, He will certainly use it with you.

Many young businessmen, businesswomen and ministers overlook this precept and try to build this favor themselves. Without the prerequisite of pleasing God, it never works out. God gives supernatural favor, and He will open doors no man can open. I have seen this favor work when, in the natural, there was no real reason to be given favor.

Several years ago, we began to do business with a very large fast-food chain, primarily in one region of the country. The chain requested that we produce some advertising materials for a new product that was being test-marketed in one of the regions.

The advertising produced such impressive results that the regional manager contacted us and asked for permission to send our name and product results to the entire chain through their voice mail system. We began receiving calls from all over the United States that day.

You cannot buy this favor for any price. God always makes a way where there seems to be no way.

Favor seems to be God's primary method of promoting His men and women. We could describe favor as an *unusual appreciation of a person to the extent that this appreciation goes far beyond the normal application.* Often, when God's favor is evident, it seems almost like there has been a long, deep friendship with the person giving favor when, in fact, you may have only known him or her a short time. Sometimes this favor will last indefinitely; in other cases, it may be temporary.

An example of long-term favor can be found in the way a relationship developed with a particular vendor. Our relationship was already healthy because of previous successful business dealings we had had. However, within a few years, our faith was tried as our business literally stood on the edge of bankruptcy. We did not choose to exercise bankruptcy, but rather decided to stand for deliverance on the scriptural principle of Isaiah 50:7: "For the Lord GOD will help me; therefore shall I not be confounded: therefore have I set my face like a flint, and I know that I shall not be ashamed."

During this testing, when our business was at its lowest ebb, we received our first order from a major fast-food chain. It was not a large order, but to fulfill the purchase, many items had to be produced in a sizable quantity. At the time, we did not have the money to produce the items due to the significant problems in our business.

My assumption was that we probably could not

obtain credit. Long ago I had learned that after prayer, you always act. You ask, you seek and you knock. I called two vendors who could have produced the materials. Their response was predictable; they were not interested in the least. Adding insult to injury, we were behind by several months on our invoice payments.

A good piece of advice that I offer through years of experience is don't quit asking when you get no for an answer. You just keep asking, seeking and knocking. Ask until you get an answer that agrees with the word of God to you. I called another vendor; a person with whom I had favor, who was one of the owners. When I explained the order and what it could mean for the future, he became very interested and decided to get involved.

God shows your potential to the person giving you favor. I have seen people present their case without explaining to the person giving favor your future potential that, in turn, will benefit them. It is not pity or benevolence that we need.

I knew the owner was aware that we had invoices from previous months that we were unable to pay, so I offered to let his company handle all the billing and receive the funds before we got our portion. After a few seconds of silence on the phone, he said, "Mike, you send the orders, and I'll ship the merchandise, period. You do the billing and pay me when you get paid." Over the next few months he shipped several thousands of dollars of merchandise for us.

You might ask, "Why did he grant you favor?" I do not really know, except I know it was God working through this man that brought help to me in a real time of need. You also might ask, "Well, what did he get out of it?" Of course he received some business from us for many years. Much more valuable, I suspect, was the fact that he unknowingly participated in a spiritual law in which God says: "*He who blesses you, I will bless.*" I have seen, even to the date of the writing of this book, his business grow and grow, and today my benefactor has a large, blessed business.

God has given us great favor with our clients, vendors, shippers and even with the IRS. When we do not know God as deeply as we should, we will always underestimate His ability. When we recognize that we are in Christ and He is in us, He has been made wisdom to us (1 Cor. 1:30). The wisdom we can impart to our clients is invaluable, and usually will make the difference between the success and failure of a project.

The book of Daniel tells the story of the prophet Daniel and King Nebuchadnezzar. In Daniel 1:9 the prophet tells us: "Now God had brought Daniel into favor and tender love with the prince of the eunuchs." Daniel and three of his friends had refused the king's feast and had chosen to eat simple food instead. The results of the decision are recorded in verse 17: "As for these four children, God gave them knowledge and skill in all learning and wisdom: and Daniel had understanding in all visions and dreams."

What an awe-inspiring report, and what a blessing!

Verse 20 reveals: "And in all matters of wisdom and understanding, that the king enquired of them, he found them ten times better than all the magicians and astrologers that were in all his realm." Christians often read this verse and apply it only to Daniel and to the time he wrote the scripture.

No, thank God, it is not just for Daniel, but it is for you and me as well! If He ever did it for one, He will do it for another if they meet the same conditions. He is even doing it today. *We are an answer, not a problem.* You see, God wants to use you and the wisdom he has imparted to you. Faith obtains the promise, like any other blessing that God has for His children.

Daniel 2:47–48 shows God's continued favor in Daniel's life: "The king answered unto Daniel, and said, Of a truth it is, that your God is God of gods, and a Lord of Kings, and a revealer of secrets, seeing thou couldest reveal this secret. Then the king made Daniel a great man, and gave him many great gifts, and made him ruler over the whole province of Babylon, and chief of the governors over all the wise men of Babylon."

In one day God can promote you from a prison to a palace.

We have to apply the principles and methods that God used in biblical times to today's situations. Often we have an answer for a complex problem in our spirit man, but we have not been trained to discern the work of the Holy Spirit taking place within us. He not only knows spiritual things, but *all* wisdom and understanding are His. He can reveal technical, business or political wisdom. He is not limited to the area of ministry that we would call "church affairs."

Having answers to complex situations in business will open doors of favor that could not be opened any other way.

Chapter Five

Divine Appointments

NOT ONLY WILL GOD REVEAL HIS SECRETS TO HIS children and give them wisdom beyond anything the world has to offer, He will make appointments for them to meet the right people. Once I felt led to call on a major oil company at their regional headquarters. I had no natural signs that anyone there would want to see me. We had developed a few minor items for them at a local service station several months before but heard nothing from them.

I flew into the city early one morning, rented a car and drove to the regional office. Honestly, I felt a little silly calling on a major oil company without so much as an appointment. I usually would not do such a thing, but then it seemed as if the Lord had directed me to do it. I gave my business card to the receptionist on the tenth floor and asked for the operations manager. In a couple of minutes the receptionist returned from presenting my card and asked if I could wait a few minutes. I agreed to wait and thought within myself, "This is at least an encouragement."

In a few minutes, two gentlemen came out, greeted me, and introduced themselves as the operations

manager and an associate. They informed me that
they had been talking about me earlier that morning
and were surprised to find me at their office.
Naturally, I thought they had me mixed up with
someone else because I had never met either of them,
and this was several hundred miles from our location.

As we walked into their offices, they asked if my
firm was the one that had developed the items for their
service stations a few months earlier. I said *yes*, and
they began to tell me what they wanted to do with all
of their service stations in Florida.

They asked me if I could do it and how much would
it cost. I responded by asking for a calculator and
promptly figured a price. Once I presented the price,
they immediately had the secretary type up some purchase orders for me. I walked out with a briefcase full
of orders and started a good relationship with a major
oil company.

Several years ago, God spoke an overwhelming
word to my spirit. I was not even thinking about the
subject. Suddenly, I heard the voice of the Lord in my
heart as He spoke these words to me: "Son, I'm going
to give you the (I'll omit the name of the company for
the sake of confidentiality) account."

This account is one of the largest advertisers in the
world. They are active in nearly all countries around
the globe. What a staggering declaration from God!
But then, we have an awesome God! I was shocked
when, just out of the blue, God spoke a word and simply said, "I'm going to give you this account."

You might ask, "Why does God speak in advance?"
Although God speaks and you hear, you still have to use
faith to receive His promises and to grow, and we must
grow into the ability to handle what God gives us.

It was a huge account. At the time God spoke those
words, I had only one employee. But that didn't stop
God. Growth was in His plan.

We have to increase the size of our buckets to match what God says He is going to do. After many years of learning to listen to the voice of the Lord, I also have learned to ask God to confirm what I believe He has spoken so as to prevent misunderstanding of what He said. In this case I felt I should write to the vice president of the division we would most likely deal with first. I wrote a pleasant introductory letter and got an unexpected reply, *absolutely nothing.* One must be certain that you have heard the voice of the Lord and not some other spirit speaking. Yet, I knew the Lord had spoken, so I prayed for God to confirm His word in His way.

He did!

Several months later, we received a call from a contact in New Orleans. My contact was in a marketing position with a fast-food chain there. He asked if I would come to visit their company and meet with several people about doing work for them.

Of course, I said *yes,* and he said he would let me know when to come.

Once I hung up the phone, I knew I should prepare to go within a day or two, but I really didn't want to go that week, so I didn't make any arrangements.

On Thursday afternoon, I received a call informing me that the best time to meet would be Friday at 10:00 A.M.

It has always been my practice to negotiate very good airfares, but I could not barter for a bargain to New Orleans on such a short notice. After being on the phone too long trying to save a little on airfare, my wife said, "Just quit it! You know God wants you there! Just order the ticket and go!" Not only did God give me the Holy Spirit, but he also gave me a helpmate to speak for Him when I would not listen to His words directly.

I had to fly through Atlanta to get to New Orleans. On the flight from Atlanta to New Orleans, I sat by a couple from Atlanta and noticed that they knew the couple in the seats right in front of us. As we talked, I learned that they were Christians. Their church had been involved recently in building a recreation center, and the funds had not come in to pay for it. I began to quote the scripture about asking, seeking and knocking.

Immediately the man just ahead of us turned around and said, "Would you repeat that please?" I did, and he asked where the scripture was found. At the time, the exact scripture referenced had slipped my mind. That was more than just a little humbling for me.

The gentleman turned back around and said, "Oh, I apologize for not introducing myself." He told me his name and gave me his card. Of all people, *he was the vice president of the division in the company God had promised me.* I had the opportunity not only to meet him but also to talk and correspond with him.

God is still working on bringing this entire account to our company. I recently saw a check go across my desk from the company. It was a gentle reminder that when God speaks, He means it. When we believe it, speak it and act on it, He will make it happen.

Chapter Six

Attitude Determines Altitude

THERE IS A LOT OF INFORMATION ON THE MARKET TODAY about the importance of attitude, with such titles as *Attitude Is Everything, The Power of Attitude* and *Success Through a Positive Mental Attitude.*

While all the information may be good, it falls far short of the attitude God wants in His servants. The attitude God wants from us embraces two complete but seemingly opposite positions.

One position is to know that we are King's kids with all the resources of the King and His kingdom. We have and should be exercising the tremendous authority that Jesus gave us through His name.

The second position is that of a servant. Jesus said in Matthew 23:11 that whoever wants to be greatest must be the servant of all. If you want to be great, you must serve a lot of people. You have got to give more to become more.

The world has the opposite theory. They think you have to take more to have more. Nothing could be further from the truth.

In our business, we constantly are finding ways to give our customers more value, more service and more favor. It is exciting to see what God does when we do not base our motives on greed but on blessing and being of service to others. While you are trying to give more, your competition is trying to take more.

By believing God and searching for better ways to conduct our business, we actually have reduced our cost on some products as much as 50 percent within a couple of years. Now we are able to obtain superior products at a significant discount. Of course, we pass on part of the savings to our customers, and we retain a portion. In cases such as these our customer benefits, and we increase our profit margin. The attitude has to be, "There is a better way to give our customers more for less and for our company to prosper simultaneously."

Check your attitude all the time. Are you believing God for better suppliers, better methods, special rates, discounts and all the other things that will give your customer the best value? We are constantly seeking ways to improve our customer service. We want our customers to put forth the least possible effort to order from us. There is no end to where this attitude can take a company.

God is looking for those willing to become the best.

God's will is that we be the best pastor, evangelist, CEO, mechanic, secretary or any other occupation in which He has placed His people. It is not through fancy presentations or slick demonstrations that this kind of favor comes: It is "not by might, nor by power, but by My Spirit, saith the LORD of hosts" (Zech. 4:6),

Some individuals have approached our company announcing they would like to work for us and dazzle our clients. Always, I have had to tell them our business is not based on dazzling our clients. Many of our clients are the "dazzlers." To the person untrained in spiritual matters, it often looks like we just stumbled into the clients and contracts. Because we have not done what the world thinks we should, people think their way would be a better and more professional approach.

That reminds me of a Bible story.

When Samuel anointed David king of Israel, no one considered him eligible. Samuel was first shown all of David's older brothers. When he was finally introduced to young David, he immediately recognized the boy as the one whom God had chosen as king.

If man can get the glory, it does not help the kingdom of God. For God to get the glory, the situation will look foolish to the unbeliever or to the carnal Christian, yet God chose the foolish things to confound the wise of this world.

The wisdom of God has a way of reducing the complex to what's really important. One of the ways we service our clients is to take what seems to them to be a very hard situation and offer solutions.

We never say it is too hard. We do not complicate our clients' lives by throwing problems back into their laps. We solve them and implement the solution. With our resources, specifically God's wisdom, most of the complex situations become simple, or at least manageable.

One case I remember from several years ago involved an advertising agency that needed some publicity items for a particular promotion. I received a call about 5:30 P.M. that they had decided to start a promotion the day after Memorial Day, which happened to be the following Monday. They informed me that it was not only their agency that would need the items but another agency as well. We needed enough materials for one hundred twenty locations, but we only had enough for thirty-eight on our shelves. Once I realized the situation, I immediately asked God for revelation on how to fill the request.

Upon inquiring, I found out my competitor in Chicago had just enough items to meet the need. I called the agency that had placed the order and told them the situation: I did not have enough of the particular supplies, but my competitor did.

They asked me if I could purchase and ship the items. I was honest and told them they could purchase the items for the same price as our company, and if I purchased them from my competitor, I would have to add a markup. They told me to continue because they could depend on our firm to get the supplies there on time.

We had our competitor ship the items on Friday, in bulk, by Federal Express. We received them Saturday morning, repackaged them and reshipped the order that Saturday. All one hundred twenty locations had their merchandise and started their promotion on Tuesday, the day after Memorial Day.

Our words are immeasurably important when we are doing the will of God. If you talk against faith or wisdom, you will not be able to run a supernatural business.

It is absolutely—and I say this without any hesitation or reservation—*mandatory* that you speak the desired results and speak faith into every situation. I do not stay around people speaking doubt, fear or unbelief. We have to train our employees to speak right. Not all of our employees are born-again believers. However, they have learned to speak possibilities and not problems.

When you speak and meditate on the problem, it grows bigger and covers the answer, but when you speak and meditate on the answer, it grows bigger until it engulfs the problem.

Who is more equipped to solve problems than God's children? We have access to the throne room of God, and we have all the resources of the Holy Spirit who knows the hearts and souls of all men. We are in a better position to help a world that desperately needs answers and people who will not make it unless we help. What a great calling to be a Christian!

A "can-do" attitude is vital to a supernatural business. None of our employees have permission to say no until conferring with senior-level management, and most often that would be me.

A large chicken producer in Arkansas had just found out that one of the major TV news magazines was going to do a story on his company. There had been some questions about the company selling chicken to some countries that were opposing the U.S.

They needed more than two thousand American flag lapel pins. This was right in the middle of the Gulf War, and due to a surge in patriotism, it was almost impossible to find this type of item.

When customer service brought this request to me, we immediately prayed. Even though we had never done any business with this client, we felt an obligation to do everything we could to meet the need. Our feeling always has been, "If anybody can do it, we can." Why not support and sponsor this kind of attitude? We have God's help.

Customer service made several inquiries only to find dead ends. "Keep calling," I said. "They're out there somewhere."

I will admit I was surprised when they told me they had found some pins that were to arrive at customs in San Francisco that very day. If we would overnight a check, they would immediately overnight the items to our client.

You might say, "Oh, that was just coincidental." Or you might say, "You just got lucky."

I don't think so. When faith reaches out, it turns the impossible into the possible.

Most people would have given up when they discovered that the flags could not easily be found. Most would not have known what they lost. But we are not "most." We are sons of the "Most" High God. To Him be the glory!

You can never have the attitude that you have arrived. There is always room for improvement. Our advertisements never say we are the best. When you proclaim that, you set yourself up for others to prove you are wrong. Let your customers and your clients say, "They are the best."

Everything speaks. Everything you do in your business expresses to others your character. All details are important. Saying you have a Christ-centered business is no excuse for sloppy work. You must prove you are Christ-centered by the work that you do. It is our policy to have everything we do speak quality and value.

It has been our experience that service is the most important commodity, and quality follows closely behind it. Price is the third consideration, but hardly ever the first. Our attitude toward all of our clients is that we want them for a lifetime. We never look on an order as an entity within itself. We know that one client lost is not just an order lost. It may be hundreds or thousands of orders. In fact, it might just be a lifetime of business lost.

Chapter Seven

The Virtue of Patience

T HERE ARE MANY REFERENCES IN THE BIBLE TO PATIENCE. Patience is a fruit of the Spirit (Gal. 5:22–23), and history's champion of patience is Job.

Without the virtue of patience in your life as a leader, you cannot obtain good results in any business or personal transaction. God always knows if you are serious about His calling and objectives.

Patience is a vital weapon against the enemy, whether spiritual or natural.

Once faith has taken hold with regard to a particular objective or promise from God, we need patience for the undergirding of that work. Hebrews 6:12 says, "That ye be not slothful, but followers of them who through faith and patience inherit the promises." This verse shows that faith and patience are "power twins."

We are living in the "now" generation, and few think of patience as being of much value. In supernatural business, objectives are long-term, and patience is required. We look at customers or potential customers as lifetime clients. We arrange or formulate all current projects to produce lifetime results. One cultivated relationship can lead to thousands of contacts over a period of years.

Picture faith as the bridge from the place where you are now to the place where you want to be. The length of the bridge is the time it will take from the present till you reach your objective or promise. The height of the bridge is the level of the place where you are, in correspondence to the height or level of the goal you want to attain. Pillars hold the bridge up, and these pillars represent patience.

Picture yourself developing the pillars of patience through the trials you encounter on the way to the objective you wish to achieve. On significant projects there may be many trials and many forces against you, but faith and patience are primary to the development of any worthwhile achievement.

Trials do not develop faith. Trials develop patience if you succeed in coming through the trial. Faith, on the other hand, is developed by hearing and doing the Word of God. Romans 10:17 substantiates this point: "So then faith cometh by hearing, and hearing by the word of God."

If you give up in the middle of a trial and do not maintain the patience necessary to go through it, the failure actually can damage your faith and hinder you from attempting to bridge an obstacle the next time you confront a challenge. (An attitude of success has to be developed, which will be discussed in a later chapter.)

Wisdom will show you the value of patience, once you call wisdom your sister and understand your kinswoman. Patience has a quiet quality that allows you to be absolutely confident in the outcome of a situation whether it happens now or later. When faith and patience work together, they produce a peace that passes all understanding.

Patience has to be exercised in your relationship with your relatives, friends and especially your employees in a supernatural business. You have to ask God to allow you to see people as He sees them. He does not see us in our imperfection. but in the perfection of Jesus. When God spoke to Abraham, He spoke to him as if he already were the father of many, even when Abraham did not have any offspring.

God sees the finished product, the reward. He sees the harvest in planting season. He sees a special person even when the baby is still in the womb.

He starts with both the answer and the destination. What a mighty God He is! If we are going to be like Him, we, too, will speak and see things as they exist in their completion.

God shows you the ultimate destination for your business and then He starts putting the pieces together. Without the picture of the jigsaw puzzle, you won't know where the pieces fit. Without the picture or the dream, you won't have enough strength to ride out the times of trial, test or stress.

Consider patience a friend and a companion. Patience truly is a virtue and a fruit of the Spirit.

Several examples come to mind when patience is mentioned. A few years ago we received a call from a young man interning with one of our major clients. He was courteous, but always demanding, and he lacked knowledge in the specific area in which he was working.

My customer service staff came to me wanting to put a stop to his demands on their time and efforts. Most of his projects were extensive and not very rewarding financially. All of them were rush projects, needed almost immediately. They wanted to write a strong letter, letting him know exactly what his place was and the rules he had to follow.

After listening to their request, I asked them one question, "Where do you think this young man will be in ten years?"

They didn't know. I suggested we consider the answer to that question before we wrote the letter they wanted to write. I encouraged them to have patience and to look on the young man as a potential executive with the corporation.

I don't have the space to tell you all that has happened since then, but here are a few highlights. For starters, within two years they made him assistant to the vice president of marketing. He has routinely passed on insight and information to us that was not available anywhere else and has since become the international marketing coordinator. I recently asked the customer service people if they still wanted to write that letter.

In this case, wisdom saw potential in this young man and encouraged patience to work with him until his potential could be reached.

Patience will help you to stay focused. You won't be giving up one day and starting again the next. Patience is a stabilizer.

Many promises Donna and I received concerning supernatural business are just now coming to fulfillment after fifteen or more years.

God also will work with you for years to build the foundation necessary to support your business. If you build without this foundation and without God, whatever you build will not last. Jesus said in Matthew 7:24–27, "Therefore whosoever heareth these sayings of mine, and doeth them, I will liken him unto a wise man, which built his house upon a rock: And the rain descended, and the floods came, and the winds blew, and beat upon that house; and it fell not: for it was founded upon a rock. And everyone that heareth these sayings of mine, and doeth them not, shall be likened unto a foolish man, which built his house upon the sand: And the rain descended, and the floods came, and the winds blew, and beat upon that house; and it fell: and great was the fall of it."

As this illustration shows, you have to build on the rock. Rock is hard, and it takes time to build on it.

God can move you from a seemingly insignificant place to prominence in a day. He moved Joseph from prison to the position of prime minister in a day.

God moved Daniel from the lion's den to a leadership position in a day.

God moved the three Hebrew children from a fiery furnace to highly favored positions in Babylon in a day.

He can move you from where you are to a privileged position in a day.

He has to do a work *in* you in order to do a work *through* you. God is a long-term developer. He has no ninety-day wonders in His kingdom.

Put patience on your "very important" list.

Chapter Eight

Determination Prevents Extermination

WITHOUT THE VIRTUE OF DETERMINATION, YOU WILL not accomplish much in God's kingdom.

Determination comes from the heart of man. It is a root within us. You can see it in those who are *not* born again. They may be headed down the wrong road, but they are determined.

Determination is an act of the will. You can determine a lot of things. You can determine to win. You can even determine to win souls. You can determine to achieve a particular objective. You can determine to do the will of God. When linked with faith and patience, determination is an extremely powerful force. To my way of thinking, determination seems to be the first step toward success.

The Gospel of Mark tells the story of a man sowing seeds. Scripture notes that some of the seed sprang up quickly, but when the sun and wind came upon them, the plants withered because they did not have deep roots.

In my opinion, this is an allegory for a lack of determination.

In simple terms we can describe this as observing the options, making a choice and sticking with that choice. There is an inward strength that builds when we are determined.

Several years ago we were called on to design and produce a special package of promotional materials for twenty client locations in Hartford, Connecticut. We were to supply ten locations at first and a month later supply the other ten. It was an extensive project involving a large amount of materials. We were testing to learn the effectiveness of outdoor promotion materials without any other advertisement.

We shipped the materials to the locations and had them installed. They created an enormous impact on sales and customer traffic, and the test results immediately attracted the attention of the national office. A team was sent from the client's national headquarters to videotape and prepare a presentation for distribution to the entire chain.

About five days before the video team was to arrive, a hurricane-like storm swept through the Hartford area and destroyed most of the materials we had on display. The folks in Hartford were determined to continue with the promotion, and we responded with equal enthusiasm.

Although it looked impossible, we were determined to replace all of the materials and have them installed in time to do the video shoot. We were shipping packages by air to Hartford, almost on an hourly basis.

The results were astounding. Sales increased no less than 10 percent at each location, and the daily customer count increased significantly. The last ten locations duplicated the results of the first ten. This project resulted in our company becoming a leader in the chain with which we were working.

Determination is a powerful force and a major root of strength.

Chapter Nine

Perseverance

WHILE DETERMINATION WORKS HAND-IN-HAND WITH perseverance, the two are definitely different.

Perseverance is the ability to withstand enemies, no matter how hard the going gets. The age-old cliché, "When the going gets tough, the tough get going," can be used to illustrate perseverance. The force of perseverance, which is anchored so firmly in my soul, says circumstances cannot get hard enough to make me quit. An attitude like that of a soldier is often necessary in dealing with tough situations. When you are in for the long haul, you will see battles and obstacles as "no big problem."

Not too long after our faith walk began, we encountered an attack like we had never experienced before. After fulfilling what we thought was the will of God, there was a general economic downturn, and our business just seemed to stop. A major lawsuit was filed against our business. At the time we didn't understand why we were encountering such a challenge. Much of the time needed to build the business was now spent responding to the legal situation. Everything I was doing seemed unproductive.

After much prayer, we decided to go on the offensive. Then things began to change.

Donna and I fortified our determination that with God, we were tough enough to handle the situation. We took it one day at a time. I decided I would treat the situation as a chess game. Donna and I actually began to enjoy the challenges that were presented to us as we mounted a strong offensive. We knew God was with us, and we were going to win.

We did win. Thank God, circumstances did not destroy us. God refined our faith in the heat of that trial, and a foundation stone was formed for the future.

When we put together perseverance, determination, faith and patience, they combined to create a powerful force. In the past, I had looked defeated and angry when I encountered the opposing side. But now I began to smile and look like a winner all the time. That was not easy. There was a lot of pain, but it yielded great dividends. With God's help, we turned Satan's attack against us into a victory for God's Word.

Once you know these principles, you should never again be intimidated in this area. When a trial comes your way, it can do one of two things: 1) It can destroy you if you are not established in the Word of God, or 2) Your faith in God can destroy it. If you are established in the Word, you can overcome the situation. Satan will have no place there and cannot successfully use the same circumstances in the future.

Many things were not pleasant during that time of testing, but Donna and I learned to persevere. We rejoiced when we did not feel like it. We counted it all joy, and it eventually became joy. If you know, like the apostle James, that the trying of your faith works patience, then let patience have her perfect work. You will become complete, wanting nothing.

Wow! What a foundation was being built! God was

preparing us for the future. We had a vision, we had Jesus and we were willing to pay the price for success in Him.

Chapter Ten

Vision and Destination

"WHERE THERE IS NO VISION, THE PEOPLE PERISH: but he that keepeth the law, happy is he" (Prov. 29:18).

If you do not know where you are going, you probably won't get there. If nowhere is your destination, you are already there.

I have a problem with someone, no matter how old or young, rich or poor, male or female, educated or uneducated, who does not have a vision. Beyond the large vision that God gives for particular individuals, you should have a vision for every area of your life.

In Hebrews 11:1 we find, "Now faith is the substance of things hoped for." I like to paraphrase it by saying, "Faith is the substance of things envisioned."

Without vision or hope there is nothing in which to place our faith. Hope or vision is a blueprint for faith. Without the blueprint, faith does not have a plan. It is very important that you, with the help of the Lord, develop a vision for your life and in every area of your life.

Within our corporation, we are constantly designing for the future. When visions are expressed, the people and the pieces come together. Many times God has spoken to my heart and given me prophetic words concerning the future.

His words have described a vision for the future and planted a picture of it in my heart. Most of the time, I do not know how something is going to happen. It doesn't matter. It will happen if I am faithful and add action to my faith, for the Scripture says in James 2:20, "But wilt thou know, O vain man, that faith without works is dead?"

Without proper action on our part, faith does not work. Once we seek God's wisdom in applying the vision, He will begin to reveal how to accomplish it—and rarely will it be the way the world would do it.

Some time ago I was watching a program on Trinity Broadcasting Network. One of the teachers on the program made a statement that grabbed my attention. It did not seem all that profound at the time, but it stayed in my mind. He said, "Funding follows vision." I began to meditate on that and realized that if our vision in business was to be accomplished, we had to share it.

Following up on my vision, I met with two major document machine manufacturers and shared the vision of our company with them. I was excited over our opportunities and described my perceptions to them. I explained that I wanted to get on the leading edge of technology and that I wanted them to let me know what equipment they offered. I was not concerned about our ability to buy the equipment at the time, but I wanted to know exactly what was available.

I was definitely excited by what happened next. Within three weeks, each manufacturer had delivered its latest piece of graphics equipment to our design center for our evaluation and trial. One had a very low-cost development program for six months to allow time for the business to refine the use of the machine. If this had been the extent of the matter, it would have been fine, but God's desires for our prosperity exceed ours. In Deuteronomy 8:18 we find the real purpose of prosperity, "But thou shalt remember the LORD thy God: for it is He that giveth thee power to get wealth, that He may establish his covenant which He sware unto thy fathers, as it is this day." God is interested in establishing and proving His covenant.

Beyond the vision, there is a door of opportunity. If we step through the door by faith, we find a panorama of opportunities and options previously unknown to us. In the next chapter, I describe the panorama of opportunities and events that unfolded when we stepped through a door that was opened to us.

Our humanity cannot imagine what God has prepared for His children. Because of this we fall far short of accomplishing and fulfilling the desires and wishes of our heavenly Father.

Oh, if we could dream and meditate with the Lord of glory! There is no limit in God. We are the limiters, if there is a limit. It must be sad to our heavenly Father to have prepared so much for us and we—through fear, misunderstandings, wrong doctrine and all such nonsense—fall far short of even attempting to fulfill His dreams for our lives.

We are told just how much is given to us in 2 Peter 1:3: "According as His divine power hath given unto us all things that pertain unto life and godliness, through the knowledge of Him that hath called us to glory and virtue." I believe this means what it says: He has given us everything that relates or pertains to life and godliness.

You may say, "Oh yes, but I was born handicapped," or "I am a minority." Some may say, "I don't even know who my father or mother is."

That is what is so great about working with the Lord—He is no respecter of persons. He knew where you were going to be born. He knew what the conditions would be, and yet He loved you enough to prepare a destination just for you.

Sometimes I think about our leaders and how they began life. The Reverend E. V. Hill of Los Angeles was born and raised in a little two-room house. Yet he is a man of such vision that many presidents have invited him to the White House. Brother Hill is a welcomed dignitary of God all over the world.

Pat Robertson started a worldwide television network, the Christian Broadcasting Network, and did not even own a television set. What a great God we serve!

Paul and Jan Crouch believed God for $35,000 to cover the balance of a down payment on their first television station. The money came, but not until fifteen minutes before the deadline. Now Trinity Broadcasting Network spans the entire world.

When I think of distinguished leaders, I always think of my friend, the late Reverend John Osteen. He left a successful missionary career to return to Houston, Texas, to pastor a little congregation of less than two hundred. His ministry expanded to more than one hundred countries and, even after his homegoing, continues to influence thousands of other ministries.

The grace of God and the abundance of His blessings are truly overwhelming!

All of these men and women of God had a vision. All of them took a first step toward their vision, and every time, God opened a panorama of opportunities and events that was not evident when they took that first step.

God's pattern is always vision, faith, action, confirmation and fulfillment, in that order.

If He did it for the men and women of the Bible, and if He does it for the men and women of God today, cannot we expect Him to do it for us?

One of my greatest goals in writing this book is to encourage and motivate others to attempt the impossible. I want to help people become everything God has planned for them and see them go beyond the normal mundane thinking of our time, which often leaves out faith in God and sometimes even denies His very existence.

Chapter Eleven

Nuggets of Wisdom

G OD GAVE ME TWO DISTINCT WORDS that have opened up a whole new horizon of vision.

One of the words was, "Get your business on the leading edge of technology." The other was, "partnership with major corporations."

Those were very unusual words for our business.

God gave technology to us all to bless the world, not to curse it. He would give it to the Christian first if there were one in that particular field who would "run with it."

Upon receiving these words, I researched the two leading manufacturers of document machines that I referenced earlier. The real nugget was to follow.

One of the machines was a high-speed, high-volume color laser printer. Once we were able to begin using this unit in our design center, it allowed us to produce full-color catalogs and brochures in a matter of hours or days in comparison with the weeks and months previously required. As we began to see the potential of using this piece of equipment, we relayed our enthusiasm to the national sales manager of the company.

The manager actually visited with us at our center, and we surprised him with the number of different ways we were using the machine. A relationship developed, and the company asked us if we were willing to be featured in a national advertising campaign for the product. Naturally, we agreed, and the campaign was very successful. The company mailed out around a hundred thousand direct-mail pieces.

If that were the end of the story, it would have been fine, but that was not the end. It was just the beginning.

The sales manager recommended that we send a letter and samples to the advertising staff at the company's national office. We did, and a vendor relationship developed with this sizable client. We believe, in due season, there will be great rewards from this action.

The second word I received from the Lord was "partnership with major corporations."

I will admit this was a rather strange word, as our company is certainly not the size of any of these major corporations. That is the main reason it is so much better to be working with the Lord. He knows what He is doing and how it will work out in the end.

Since receiving this word, we have entered a partnership with several large corporations. The major corporations have the resources and the clients, and our company has innovation, enthusiasm and the ability to do things very quickly. We became "good leaven" to our business partners. God said, "He who blesses you, I will bless." This has turned out to be a mutually beneficial situation with these large enterprises.

There are no losers in God's plan except Satan. If you are going to be used in God's supernatural business and be a winner, you need to see yourself and your business as a blessing to others. You can be a blessing to your employees, vendors, clients and most of all, to the kingdom of God by giving as God directs.

Chapter Twelve

Confession Brings Possession

THERE ARE MANY BOOKS DEDICATED EXCLUSIVELY TO confession and the power of words. Confession is absolutely one of the most critical areas to the success of a supernatural business.

You cannot cooperate with God and His plan and simultaneously talk against it. Words are extremely powerful and can move a company one way or the other. The words spoken by President John F. Kennedy, "We will place a man on the moon in this decade," became the motivator and set the stage for the event to actually take place.

When one who is in authority speaks the desired results in powerful action words, this act begins to move mountains and people. Believers must realize the authority they have been given in Christ.

The New Testament book of James states that the tongue is the rudder of the ship. If we are going to steer our ship to success, important words are going to have to be spoken.

Words express vision. People see vision through words and begin to act in harmony.

Through words, we set goals. Our goals are the targets at which we can direct our efforts constructively and in harmony with others.

Words also are the outward expression of thought and intent. The Bible says in Matthew 12:34, "For out of the abundance of the heart the mouth speaketh." Matthew 12:37 reads, "For by thy words thou shalt be justified, and by thy words thou shalt be condemned."

There is no way we can possibly overstate the importance of words. It is vital to the success of our business endeavors to always speak the desired result, not the problem. Voicing the problem simply serves to establish it as a formidable obstacle. According to the Word of God, speaking the answer diminishes the problem and causes appropriate action to be taken to correct or overcome the situation. Mark 11:23 reveals: "For verily I say unto you, that whosoever shall say unto this mountain, be thou removed, and be thou cast into the sea; and shall not doubt in his heart, but shall believe that those things which he saith shall come to pass; he shall have whatsoever he saith."

We are to speak to the mountain. If we speak to the mountain and do not doubt but believe that what we say will happen, the mountain will be removed. This principle is powerful yet so simple that many Christians will not attempt it. Many will pray that *God* will remove the mountain, but they will not act on the authority that He already has given them through their words.

If you listen to the world as described on the six o'clock news, it is easy to feel discouraged and defeated. Sometimes things look hopeless, and consequently we do not act. If you begin to speak words of defeat and hopelessness, Satan is more than happy to oblige you in helping to accomplish that which you have spoken. He is looking and listening for an avenue into your affairs. Speaking words of defeat gives him the authority to enter the situation.

In contrast, words spoken in alignment with the Word of God allow the Holy Spirit and the angels of God to become involved in our affairs. It is very exciting to actually realize that God desires to be involved in this way.

Early in our business a situation occurred where the words spoken were so critical that I believe they could have stopped everything that is happening today.

We had been asked to develop a small catalog of our products for a client. We were working in only one region and only on a small scale. Yet, I knew God was working to take our business to the national level. He had spoken this to me, and it was in the process of developing.

I had received an inquiry from a large client during May of that year and had responded by attending a meeting at its national headquarters. We had agreed on a small catalog, and they were about ready to send it to all of their franchisees and representatives.

After several trips and discussions, the catalog was ready for printing except for the layout of one item. I had given several suggestions, but we had not agreed on the wording.

We had worked on the project since May, but November came, and a decision had not yet been made on the product's description. One weekend I suddenly had the greatest temptation to speak words against the project. I wanted desperately to say these words to my wife, "Honey, this is like most of the other projects in the past. They start off great, but they just fizzle out and turn into puff."

That temptation plagued me all weekend. It was greater than any other temptation I remember encountering. Even though my flesh wanted to say those words, I would look at Donna and say, "Honey, this is going to be the best financial blessing that has ever happened to us."

During that weekend I quoted relevant scriptures and required my mouth to agree with God's desire to bless His people. I realized on Sunday evening I had overcome the temptation. I had not given in to my flesh. I had not spoken against God's Word, and I had the victory.

On Monday, around 9 A.M., I heard the voice of the Lord say to me, "Call your business office." When I did, the receptionist informed me that I had just received a call from the corporate headquarters. I returned the call and was greeted with, "Mike, do you have your pencil ready? Here is what we want to say on that item; and can you have the catalogs ready by Christmas?" Of course, I said yes and shipped three thousand catalogs by air freight to their office on Christmas Eve. They added a cover letter and mailed out the catalogs January 6.

In the next two months we received orders from virtually every state in the union. Even though these were just small orders at first, practically overnight we became a national company.

I truly believe that if I had allowed my flesh the latitude of speaking against God's will and His Word, none of this would have taken place, and all that has followed from it would not have happened.

Words are very powerful, and they determine our destiny.

I have learned to speak powerful words over my employees. I have heard people say, and I am sure you have, too, "You sure can't find good help these days.

You just can't get dependable workers. They're just looking for a paycheck."

These and other similar words serve to prevent you from finding good employees. I prefer to speak words such as, "My employees are the best in the business. God brings good employees our way. They all give at least 110 percent."

Once you begin to speak these types of words over your employees, you begin to see it actually happening. God's Word works in employees as well as everywhere else.

Good words reflecting God's will and Word should be spoken over all aspects of your business. I constantly speak that we have the best clients in the business, that they always pay their bills promptly and give us favor in every situation.

Several years ago, a large franchisee of one of the chains we serve was in a financial bind and heading toward bankruptcy. We continued to sell to them on an open account long after we should have stopped. I should have caught it but did not.

By the time I realized they were in serious trouble, they owed us more than ten thousand dollars, which was quite a large sum at the time. The comptroller of the corporation called and expressed his regrets for having to file bankruptcy under Chapter eleven, which allows for reorganization.

I immediately began to speak good words over their company. Rather than complaining and fussing over the money I was apparently going to lose, I expressed our genuine appreciation for their business and offered to help in any way we could. I encouraged them to continue to order from us on a cash basis.

I am sure this was in contrast to many of their suppliers. Not only did this company pull out of the bankruptcy but they also paid us every dollar they owed us and continue to be our client even to this day. We have received many thousands of dollars from that company since. I could have complained and fussed and maybe never collected the money they owed us at the time of their difficulty.

Positive confession helped lead them out of debt and helped us collect what they owed us. Both of us were blessed!

We retain attorneys to handle contracts and the legal facets of our business, but to this day we have never sued anyone for the collection of a debt. I truly feel a lawsuit should be the very last resort. Many companies threaten legal action at the drop of a hat. Immediately the party who owes the money becomes an adversary.

Most of the businesses I have dealt with were honest and desired to pay their bills. In a few cases I have just called the client and explained that if they could not pay their debt, we would write it off. I have always added that we valued their previous business, and their relationship with us was worth more than a few dollars.

This may sound like I am naïve, but if you are listening to God, it is not. This policy has resulted in a bad debt write-off of less than one-half of one percent of sales, and we are working to improve that figure.

Once you have decided to speak God's words over your business, the difference in your outlook will surprise you, and this is no small decision. It is a major change in perspective.

I never use the words; "We cannot afford something." I may decide not to do something because it is not wise or prudent, but not because I cannot afford it. We can afford to do anything God speaks or allows in His Word for us to do. None of the words you are reading here are to be taken as arrogant or prideful. Once you understand the true purpose of proper confession and the power of your words, you will want to apply yourself in this area. Positive confession is one of the most important lessons to learn in life. There are some excellent books on the market concerning this subject, and I encourage anyone to study and practice these principles.

These are some examples of the confessions Donna and I use over our life, ministry and business, which you also might want to employ:

> This is the day the Lord hath made; we will rejoice and be glad in it.
>
> He hath not given me the spirit of fear, but of power and of love and of a sound mind.
>
> Thank God, I have the mind of Christ. The truth of God abides in me, and He teaches me all things.
>
> My ways please the Lord; therefore I have the favor of God and man.
>
> I lean not on my own understanding, In all my ways I acknowledge the Lord, and He directs my path.
>
> I have pity on the poor, therefore I shall never lack.
>
> The joy of the Lord is my strength.
>
> No weapon formed against me shall prosper, and every tongue that rises against me in judgement shall be condemned.
>
> I can do all things through Christ who strengthens me.

Chapter Thirteen

Ego,
The Business Killer

THE ORIGINAL SIN WAS AN ATTEMPT BY SATAN TO EXALT himself above God. Defeat has always followed self-promotion, then and now. Scripture says that God resists the proud but gives grace to the humble (James 4:6). There is always the temptation to think of ourselves as the source of accomplishment.

If in your business or ministry you begin to take credit for achieving or building, then you are in for a fall. Many well-intentioned people have tried to give me credit for the accounts we have. In each case, I have quickly announced that it was not I but the move of the Holy Spirit working to bring us success.

Much of the time their response has been, "Yes, but you had to do your part." That is true, but not in the way most want to give man credit.

We do have a part, but it is only to follow God's direction. All of the glory has to be given to God. Yes, His presence will bring His glory on the scene, and it is glorious, *but it is not our glory.*

79

It is very humbling to see God doing great things and using some of us who are the most unlikely to succeed, in man's view. Scripture cautions us to be very careful when we have gained success or prosperity lest we forget God who gave us the power to get wealth.

I have watched as many companies, both large and small, fell into the ego trap.

There was once a very good, and profitable, small airline. It had developed a niche in the market in the South. Each quarter the airline consistently showed a nice profit. It was growing steadily, expanding its corner of the market. Suddenly, the airline announced it was going to be an international airline and began promoting and scheduling flights to Europe.

Within one year it went bankrupt. Why? Because of ego!

Recently I talked with the former general counsel for that airline. He confirmed exactly what I had observed. The decision to fly to Europe was not a carefully thought-out financial decision with the intent of making a profit, but a decision based on ego.

Many times, after experiencing significant financial success, a company's management does not mature fast enough to contend with the realms where ego will take them.

Several years ago a large computer chipmaker began to use a lot of ego-based advertising that spoke of its perfection. The company seemed invincible.

Millions of computers contained its chip. Magazine articles would point to its success and dominance in the market. The last thing on the executives' minds was a big snafu, but a professor working at a college realized that his personal computer was not giving the right answers. Upon investigation, he realized that it was actually wrong in its calculations.

The professor reported the problem to the industry, and the company snubbed everyone by announcing it would replace the chip only for those who would need to do extensive calculations.

Of course, this attitude insulted everyone who owned a computer chip of this type, and it resulted in damage to the company and its reputation.

When ego gets in the way, a fall is inevitable.

When you find yourself stretching the truth about your company or your ministry, you are probably falling into ego's trap. We want everyone to think highly of us. If we are the biggest, the best, the largest or have the most of anything, we believe others will think more favorably of us.

Actually, what we want is the approval of others. Approval does not come through ego, but from being of service to others.

Psalm 75:6–7 tells us that God knows exactly who, when and where to promote. "For promotion cometh neither from the east, nor from the west, nor from the south. But God is the judge: he putteth down one, and setteth up another."

Once we get past the point of self-promotion, God can really use us or our company or ministry. This is not an easy area to overcome, and we have to daily crucify the motive of self-promotion.

We enjoy letting folks know that we know someone important. God looks on all men and women as important, and He wants them all to be ministered to as His children. The person or persons who may have the most impact on your life may not be someone who is well-known or is thought of as super successful.

I have watched and been involved with several ministries over the years. Most ministry leaders are sincere. However, when in the course of time a measure of success comes, some begin to change. Where once they catered to hurting men and women and seemed to have a great degree of humility, they now become self-centered. Their advertising changes. Their services change. Pride and ego show up. It is not long before these ministries are either gone altogether, or they are reduced to much less visibility.

God simply will not tolerate pride and ego in our lives, ministries or businesses. If it comes in, it has to go. There are no *ifs, ands* or *buts*; pride and ego have to go. It is an absolute law we find in Proverbs 16:18: "Pride goeth before destruction, and an haughty spirit before a fall."

My prayer to God the Father through Jesus Christ is this, that I would be convicted by the Holy Spirit when pride, ego or other self-aggrandizement would try to enter in.

Each morning I invite the Holy Spirit to guide me into all wisdom and ask that I would recognize His direction in all decisions that day. I have to constantly check my words and thoughts for wrong attitudes and immediately correct any that are found. I do not want to offend the Spirit of God or interfere with the angels of God ministering for my family, business, ministry or myself.

Chapter Fourteen

The Purpose of Prosperity

O NE OF THE MOST MISUNDERSTOOD PRINCIPLES IN THE entire church today seems to be the real purpose of godly prosperity.

We have an excellent example of what our priorities for wealth should be in Matthew 16:26: "For what is a man profited if he shall gain the whole world and lose his own soul? Or what shall a man give in exchange for his soul?"

The answers to these two questions from the scripture seem self-evident. Absolutely nothing is worth anything, if our soul will be lost. God values the soul of man, even just one man, above all the riches of the world. Isn't that an amazing fact?

How much do we value just one soul? How much does your church value souls? How much effort do you expend to reach souls?

These are excellent questions to begin with in the study of godly prosperity, but we need to look at more than questions. Sometimes we simply need to consider the most obvious arrangement the Lord has made for our blessing, as in Deuteronomy 8:18: "But thou shalt remember the LORD thy God: for it is He that giveth thee power to get wealth, that He may establish his covenant which He sware unto thy fathers, as it is this day."

First, we need to understand that God is good. He is all good, all the time. There is no shadow of turning in him. He does not tempt, neither tempts He any man.

When we define prosperity, we also have to define the opposite—poverty. Jesus said in John 10:10: "The thief cometh not, but for to steal, and to kill, and to destroy: I am come that they might have life, and that they might have it more abundantly."

God is a God of abundance.

Poverty kills.

Poverty steals.

Poverty destroys.

It is obvious in His creation that God is a God of unlimited abundance. His plan for man has always been abundant provision. Giving liberally is in God's character. He never runs out of anything!

Poverty does not reflect God.

Poverty takes little children and puts them to bed hungry.

Poverty takes older folks and makes them go to bed in pain and in fear of the future.

Poverty makes men and women steal and try to find relief from a hurting life. Poverty degrades men and puts them in slavery.

Poverty removes hope and vision.

When worldly men accumulate wealth, they usually squander it on themselves. Their wealth does no one any good.

Wealth gotten by evil means only produces trouble and anguish. I cannot help but despise the illegal narcotics industry. Millions are suffering, hurting in hospitals and even dead because of a few greedy men motivated by Satan to enslave people. Wealth acquired by evil men only makes them more of what they already are. Their purpose is not to help anyone except themselves. They do not care how many they hurt so long as they can have their large homes, cars, boats and airplanes.

The liquor industry also has placed untold misery upon humanity.

The cigarette industry has given millions of people lung cancer and each year cost taxpayers billions of dollars.

With the gambling industry comes crime and the hellish offer of false hope and security cloaked in the wrappings of a game of chance. States are turning to gambling for income. How foolish!

When the ungodly prosper, it does not bring good; it produces misery and problems.

It is time the church woke up to the fact that it is not God's will for the world to prosper financially while millions are lost and hurting. Shame on those who think that way. It is a deception of Satan! The Scripture absolutely convinces me that God intends that we reach out to a world with hope in our hands. We need to rightly take our place in the covenant of God with His Son, Jesus, and His seed.

When we define godly prosperity, we have to start with God's most basic (and best) gift in John 3:16: "For God so loved the world, that He gave His only begotten Son, that whosoever believeth in Him should not perish, but have everlasting life."

First, God is a lover, and then He is a giver.

He is unselfish, evidenced by the fact that He gave His *only* begotten Son. He did not just give one out of many, but He gave His only one. When Jesus came to this earth, He gave His life. Why? Because He loved.

If we truly love mankind, we will give too—*sometimes until it hurts.*

It is the purpose of godly prosperity to bless the world with the Good News and to demonstrate in words and actions that God is a God of love and abundant supply. He not only cares about our eternal destination, but He loved the world enough to give His very own Son, Jesus Christ, who paid the price so that no one on this earth has to miss out on any provision God has made for mankind.

The real purpose of prosperity in the kingdom of God is to have what we need and to be able to give. If we are going to be like our Father God, we will love. We also will give, and we will display our Father's provision by offering assistance to others to meet their spiritual, intellectual and physical needs.

In Romans 8:22 we are given an example of our kinship with all humanity. Paul writes, "For we know that the whole creation groaneth and travaileth in pain together until now."

When the godly prosper, it begins to bless everyone. When a godly man's business receives a large order or contract, he should be thinking, "Where can I plant the profits to do the most good in the kingdom of God?"

Godly prosperity gives you a public pulpit to praise God. The testimony of your life and business will change others when they find out the reason for your achievement.

You will begin to see yourself as a blessing looking for a place to happen. You are not worrying about your needs. You know your needs are taken care of, and you are looking to meet the needs of someone else.

Oh what a blessing to gain and live out these truths!

There are different attitudes toward prosperity in the kingdom of God, but remember, what you are aiming for is *godly* prosperity.

You are not trying to get. You are trying to give.

You are not cursing. You are blessing.

You are not looking for accolades. You are looking for opportunities.

You are not building your kingdom. You are building His.

You do not have to prosper to go to heaven, but your failure to prosper may keep someone else from hearing the gospel, receiving Jesus and going to heaven.

Earlier in this book I shared how God presented me with the opportunity to purchase a hundred thousand-watt radio station. I had a vision of reaching the hurting at night and blessing Christians in the daytime through that station. I knew God was in it. I had plenty of confirmation, but I did not have the million dollars to purchase the station. At the time, I did not know how to move on the deal.

I missed it, and it costs to miss God.

Oh, I am not talking about personal cost to me, though knowing you have missed Him is a personally painful realization. I am talking about the souls whom we could have won to Jesus in the years since then. It still hurts to think about lost opportunities because of a lack of financial resources. I have determined in the years since then that financial obstacles will not be a hindrance to doing God's will.

If God said *do it,* He will pay for it. It is my responsibility to do all that is within my power. God will do the rest.

There is no demon in hell, nor man, nor group of men, that can stop the work of God when you have decided to do God's will and won't take *no* for an answer.

Godly prosperity is not just the state of your financial affairs; it is also an attitude. Godly prosperity is a way of thinking. Godly prosperity is a lifestyle.

You begin to think differently. I cannot relate to much of the business thinking of the world. They talk of competition and strategize about how to compete for larger and larger shares of the market. I hardly think of competition. I know that whoever wants to compete with us will have to do what we do, and they will have to know whom we know.

We build our business by giving. These principles may not agree with the philosophies of some consultants and accountants, but they work for the blessed.

I am constantly reassessing our giving to make sure we are giving sufficiently to sustain our growth. Our growth does not determine our giving. Our giving determines our growth.

This is one of the most important principles in godly prosperity. Just as a farmer plants a crop in relation to the size of harvest he expects, we give in relation to the business we expect to receive.

Why should worthy ministries not have sufficient finances?

Why should we have sick ones among us who do not receive the kind of care they need?

Why should we have little children going to bed hungry?

When men and women of God who know who they are in Christ begin to take their place and enter the prosperity that God has provided, then we will see changes. There will be no more hangups and no more justifying poverty.

We need to treat poverty like the curse that it is. We need to realize that God already has made provision for us.

As you read about my thoughts and experiences, you may have asked the question, "What kind of a man would write a book such as this?"

Well, I am just like you, hungry to do my Father's will. I am looking, and will continue to look, for ways to better please my heavenly Father and reflect His goodness to a lost and dying world.

Until Jesus comes, I intend to reach out further, expand the vision, take bigger and bolder steps, love more, give more, hear more, see more, help more, be a better husband, father, son, minister, teacher, writer, businessman, and to finally hear these words: "Well done, thou good and faithful servant."

May the Lord of Glory bless you.

THE BEGINNING

To Contact the Author:

Mike Floyd
P.O. Box 3266
Tallahassee, Florida 32315
Phone: (850) 562-4564
Email: mfloyd@altrua.com